THAUMIEL; T͟I
DIVIDED ONES

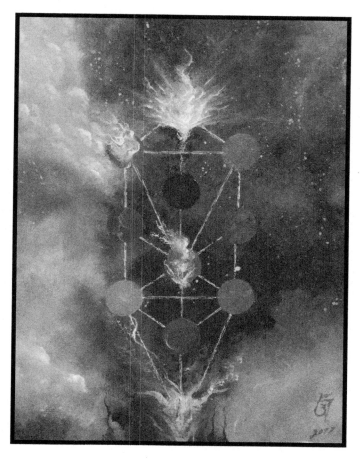

Thaumiel; The Dark Divided Ones

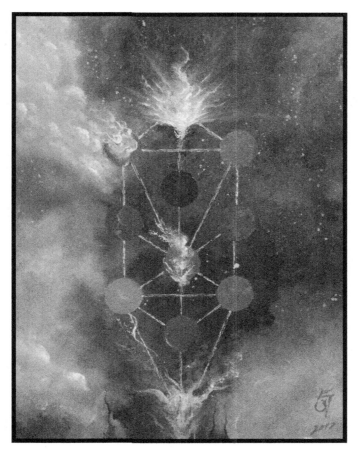

S. Ben Qayin

From The Ashes Publishing 2017

Credits

Author: S. Ben Qayin

Publisher: From The Ashes Publishing

Artwork: Carlos Andres

ISBN 978-0-692-10277-0

Acknowledgements

Firstly, I would like to give honor to my holy spiritual father, Qayin ben Samael, who has guided me upon this long and thorny path of Nod. To S. X. L. and A., I thank for their undying love and encouragement through all. This book would not have been possible without the amazing support from my spiritual family, Darcy Adsit, Jesse Garrett, Darren Taylor *(Asbjorn Torvol)* and Edgar Kerval. Thank you all for your allegiance, it means the world to me. I also would like to thank Carlos Andres for his amazing contribution of art. His interpretations of the Qliphothic realm and its inhabitants are truly transcendental. And last but by no means least, I thank The Thaumiel, Satan and Moloch for their guidance and transformation of my life while working with them, I am eternally grateful…

TABLE OF CONTENTS

"Full magical initiation is not possible without an understanding of the so-called qliphotic paths which are, in practice, as real as the shadow of any object illuminated by the sun" ~ Kenneth Grant, 'Nightside of Eden'

INTRODUCTION

"Out of the ground the Lord God caused to grow every tree that is pleasing to the sight and good for food; the tree of life also in the midst of the garden, and the tree of knowledge, of good and evil."

~ Genesis 2:9-14

The Tree of Death…of Knowledge…Exists within the hidden shadows of Qabalistic reality, in a realm known as the Sitra Ahra…the vast cold region where light is but a grey band upon the farthest horizons. The Sitra Ahra is the anathema of creation, for it lies concealed *'behind'* and *'below'* its illuminated counterpart, the realm of holiness and purity.

As a coin has two sides, we see a duality here that exists and is represented in the form of Light and Darkness which oppose one another, but nevertheless are eternally bound as one. This is essentially the philosophy of having two opposing energetic intelligences or forces united under one all-encompassing energetic Qabalistic intelligence known only as *'Ayn'*. We find this duality in unity at the core of not only the Judaic teachings, but also within the traditions of Taoism and Zurvanism as well. Though in its obscurity and being contrary to popular belief, it can also be found within the Christian bible,

"I form the light, and create darkness; I make peace, and create evil; I am the Lord that doeth all these things." ~ Isa. 45:7

"The Lord hath made every thing for His own purpose, Yea, even the wicked for the day of evil." ~ Prov. 16:4

This theory is artfully mirrored in the Taijitu symbol known more commonly as the Yin and Yang symbol.

3

This perspective embodies the idea of the personification of the eterna waring forces of Order and Chaos *(Light and Darkness)*. These forces ar as a scale that never finds rest, the balance constantly being shifted from one side to the other.

"We thus come to a notion that played a major role, not only in Sefer ha-Zohar, but in later Kabbalah and in Hasidic thought: namely, that a spark of the divine light shines even in evil. There is no complete separation between the two realms: evil has no existence as pure evil, a the polar opposite of the good; on the contrary, the two realms are interlaced." ~ Gershom Scholem

These waring forces of Order and Chaos are evenly matched; One forc rises up over aeons of time gaining control, only to have the opposin force in turn rise up to push it back down. One force can neve completely dominate the other. It is an eternal ebb and flow, so chang can never cease in the Consensual Reality Matrix and experience neve end. This cycle is eternal. It is as playing chess against yourself, only t stalemate match after match. The forces of Chaos and Order are equa Though, calm between these two forces can never be known, now tha the proverbial boat has begun to rock, they are set into perpetual motior It is a game of tug of war that produces no victor.

These forces of Chaos and Order are generally assigned the description and position of 'Good and Evil'. However, this description is made from the viewpoint of one of the two perspectives *(Chaos or Order)*, making it short sided and a limited concept. When one views the duality that exists as a whole, counteracting each other equally as one working machine/system/program, one can see that neither of these forces are *'good or evil'*. When one combines warm water with cold water, neither forces are good or evil. A forest fire could be seen as evil, destroying all life. But, it is needed every so often to cleanse the land and provide nutrients and space for new growth to occur. It is an endless cycle of destruction and rebirth. It is continuous change. It is continuous experience. And truly, neither are good nor bad, for darkness cannot exist without light, and light not without darkness.

"Yet, as the ancients became gradually aware that the same and not a different sun rose and set each day, so in the New Aeon man is becoming increasingly conscious of the possibility not only of exploring the other side of the Tree, but of the fact that it is merely the other side of a single entity..." ~ Kenneth Grant, 'Nightside of Eden'

This duality is reflected in the natures of the Qabalistic Tree of Life and the Tree of Death. Without going into too much detail *(as I assume one has a basic general understanding of the concept at this point in one's studies)*, the Tree of Life (Hebrew; Etz Ḥayyim, עץ חיים), is a Qabalistic representation of 'being' and 'creation', how existence came to be and its general composition. The Tree of Life includes various attributes at progressing stations, and ruling intelligences of these points. These stations are known as Sephiroth. As stated each Sephira has an attribute such as *'Severity, Compassion, Beauty and Kindness'*. Each Sephira bleed into and influence each other in various ways and combinations. The ten Sephiroth, their attributes and ruling angelic spirits are as follows:

~ Kether: *'The Crown'*
Ruling Angelic Intelligence: *Metatron*

~ Chochmah: *'Wisdom'*
Ruling Angelic Intelligence: *Raziel*

~ Binah: *'Understanding'*
Ruling Angelic Intelligence: *Tzaphqiel*

~ Chesed: *'Kindness'*
Ruling Angelic Intelligence: *Tzadqiel*

~ Gevurah: *'Severity'*
Ruling Angelic Intelligence: *Khamael*

~ Tiferet: *'Beauty'*
Ruling Angelic Intelligence: *Raphael*

~ Netzach: *'Victory'*
Ruling Angelic Intelligence: *Haniel*

~ Hod: *'Splendor'*
Ruling Angelic Intelligence: *Michael*

~ Yesod: *'Foundation'*
Ruling Angelic Intelligence: *Gabriel*

~ Malkuth: *'Kingdom'*
Ruling Angelic Intelligence: *Sandalphon*

~ Da'ath: *'Knowledge'*
Ruling Demonic Intelligence: *Choronzon*

"I made it beautiful with the multitude of its branches, and all the trees of Eden, which were in the garden of God, were jealous of it." ~ Ezekiel 31:9

THE TREE OF LIFE

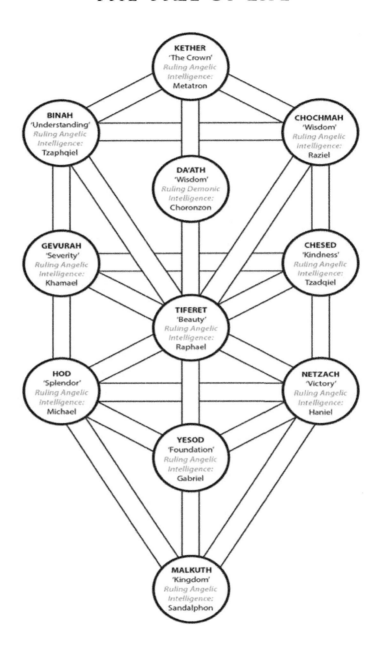

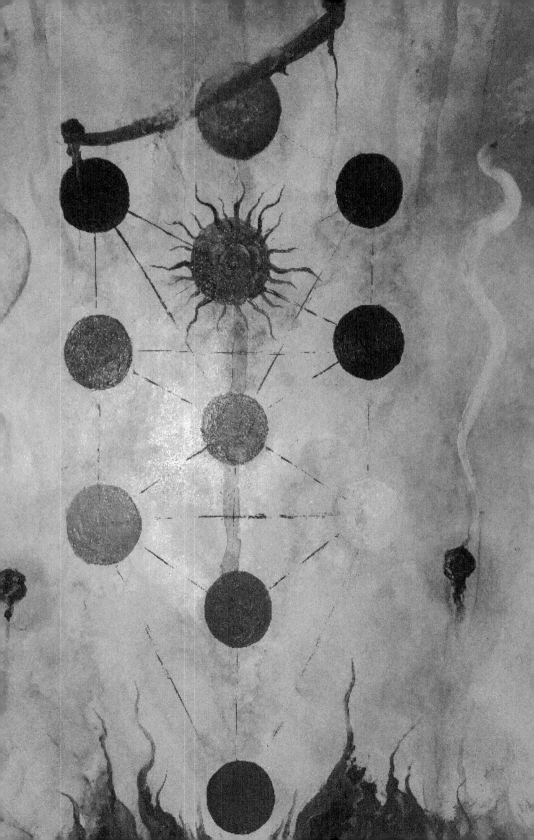

These Sephira are the emanations of creation beginning with Kether *(the crown)*, and working on down to Malkuth *(the kingdom)* through the path of the holy lightning bolt. However, there are only ten stations on the tree, the eleventh Sephira is known as a Non-Sephira, and its name is *'Da'ath'*. Da'ath it is the gateway into the realm of the Sitra Ahra, home of The Tree of Death. It exists *'In-between'* the two trees.

As the Tree of Life, the Tree of Death is comprised of ten Qliphothic spheres or husks, each with their own attributes and intelligences. They are the *'backside'* of the ten Sephira and thus, share attributes.

"The Qliphoth, Qelippot or Klippot are "the representation of evil or impure spiritual forces in Jewish mysticism." ~ 'The Book of Concealed Mystery' Translated by MacGregor Mathers

Like their counterpart the Sephira, they are laid out as follows,

~ Thaumiel: *'Duality Of God'*
Rulling Demonic Intelligence: *Satan And Moloch*

~ Ghogiel: *'The Hinderers'*
Rulling Demonic Intelligence: *Beelzebub*

~ Satariel: *'The Concealers'*
Rulling Demonic Intelligence: *Lucifuge Rofocal*

~ Agshekeloh: *'The Breakers In Pieces'*
Rulling Demonic Intelligence: *Astaroth*

~ Golohab: *'The Burners'*
Rulling Demonic Intelligence: *Asmodeus*

~ Tagiriron: *'The Disputers'*
Rulling Demonic Intelligence: *Belphegor*

~ Herab Serapel: *'Ravens Of The Burning God'*
Rulling Demonic Intelligence: *Baal/Bael*

~ Samael: *'Poison Of God'*
Rulling Demonic Intelligence: *Adrammelek*

~ Gamaliel: *'The Obscene Ones'*
Rulling Demonic Intelligence: *Lilith*

~ Lilith: *'The Whisperers'*
Rulling Demonic Intelligence: *Naahema*

THE TREE OF DEATH

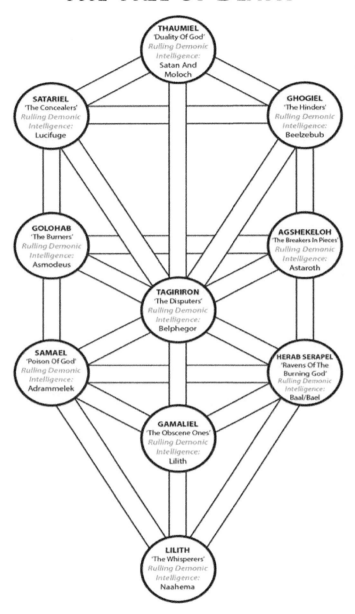

THAUMIEL
'Duality Of God'
*Rulling Demonic
Intelligence:*
Satan And
Moloch

SATARIEL
'The Concealers'
*Rulling Demonic
Intelligence:*
Lucifuge

GHOGIEL
'The Hinders'
*Rulling Demonic
Intelligence:*
Beelzebub

GOLOHAB
'The Burners'
*Rulling Demonic
Intelligence:*
Asmodeus

AGSHEKELOH
'The Breakers In Pieces'
*Rulling Demonic
Intelligence:*
Astaroth

TAGIRIRON
'The Disputers'
*Rulling Demonic
Intelligence:*
Belphegor

SAMAEL
'Poison Of God'
*Rulling Demonic
Intelligence:*
Adrammelek

HERAB SERAPEL
'Ravens Of The
Burning God'
*Rulling Demonic
Intelligence:*
Baal/Bael

GAMALIEL
'The Obscene Ones'
*Rulling Demonic
Intelligence:*
Lilith

LILITH
'The Whisperers'
*Rulling Demonic
Intelligence:*
Naahema

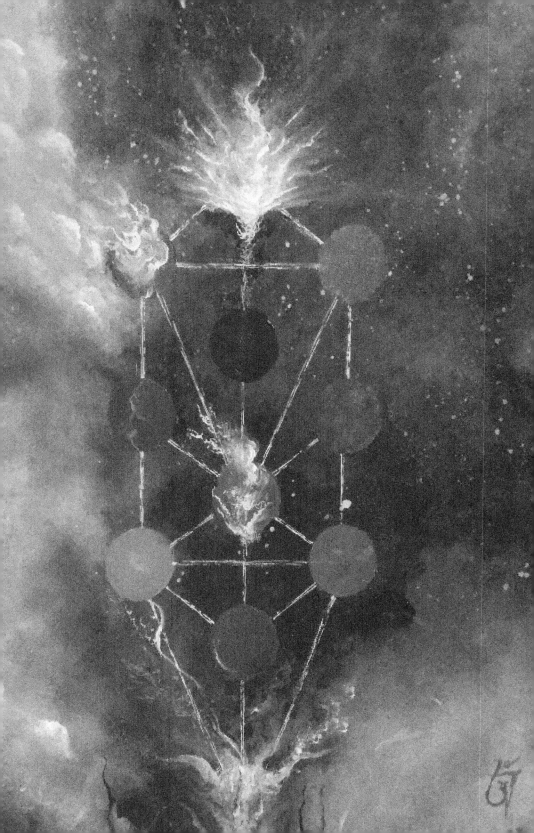

A POISON TREE

"I was angry with my friend:
I told my wrath, my wrath did end.
I was angry with my foe:
I told it not, my wrath did grow.

And I watered it in fears,
Night and morning with my tears;
And I sunned it with smiles,
And with soft deceitful wiles.

And it grew both day and night,
Till it bore an apple bright;
And my foe beheld it shine,
And he knew that it was mine.

And into my garden stole,
When the night had veil'd the pole:
In the morning glad I see,
My foe outstretched beneath the tree."

~ William Blake

Within this Qliphothic Series all eleven of the Qliphoth, their essences, ruling demonic forces and all related intelligences, are examined in absolute detail. There is much gnosis to be found within the spheres of dusk, and it is my hope to make a valuable contribution to this occult course of study within the magical community, for this age, and many more to come. The present grimoire focuses on the Qliphoth 'Thaumiel' Hebrew; אומיאל' נ, ThAVMIAL) translated as 'The Duality of God'. All related energies and intelligences of the sphere will be worked with herein. However, in order to fully comprehend this Qliphothic shell in its totality, its reverse side, the Sephira 'Kether', must first be examined.

Kether is the 'Crown', the ruling Sephira over all others, giving birth through Intent, to Chochmah; 'Wisdom', which in turn begets Binah; 'Understanding'. This holy trinity is known as the 'Supernal Triangle' and occupies the first 'world' of the Sephiroth known as 'Atziluth'. Kether is unity, singularity, containing within it (if only for an instant), all other attributes the remaining nine Sephira possess. It is the cosmic egg from which emerged separation and distinguished energies, and is appropriately known as 'The beginning of the whirlings'. As dominos (one toppling over the next), a chain reaction of division leading to awareness of self, is undergone. It is as a child that opens its pure blue eyes to the world for the first time, and begins to comprehend and add description to its surrounding reality, that ironically it itself has created. Thought/spiritual essence is set into motion that follows a logical process of division and awareness that descends the Tree of Life as a great Lightning Flash, beginning with Kether of the spiritual/Intellectual realm, on down to Malkuth, finalizing in the physical; creation, earth and matter, flesh and blood. Kether is the embodiment of divine source, it is Will or what I call Intent. It is trans-mundane divine inspiration. It is the number one, with only the placement of zero before it, nothingness. Or at least that which exists before comprehension of 'one', thus having no intrinsic value to the uninitiated mind. Kether is the first spark of all creation, all becoming, all existence. Kether 'Is'.

15

Adversely, on the Tree of Death we have opposite the position o Kether; Thaumiel, the Qliphothic sphere of duality. Thaumiel oppose the perfection of singularity, by tearing it in *two*. As Kether is unity Thaumiel is separation,

"Instead of God's unity, the dark path offers a dynamic duality as the highest principal. Unity is equivalent with extinction, while the outermost duality gives life and energy." ~ Thomas Karlsson, 'Qabalah Qliphoth and Goetic Magic'

And that is precisely the point, rather than becoming one with the Go Head, thus ending one's individual journey/experience, Thaumiel reject the absorption that occurs at this level *(in relation to Kether)* and exist outside of holy creation. Now a new path must be traversed, beyond th limits of what the Sephira allow to exist. True individuality and freedon exist within this realm, unrestrained by righteous laws that restrict.

The rebelliousness of the Tree of Death is its foundation. Th drive for separation, thus individuality, is the fueling fire which move this force into existence *'outside'* of *(or removed from)* God and it controlling influence. Anything not *'of God'* or connected *'to God'* was/is considered *'Evil'*,

"According to the Kabbalists, this act of separation made the world of human experience become coarse and material. It is obvious that this conception transfers the Tree of Knowledge of Good and Evil entirely t the side of evil, which probably explains why such a profound and influential interpretation was often held by other Kabbalists to be too radical. The latter tried to posit this same primordial harmony in the Tree of Knowledge itself: a harmony that was only destroyed by the ras and untimely separation of the fruit from the tree, whose detachment

16

from its source brought about its destruction. The symbolism perceived in the tale of Paradise varies from one account to another; what is common to all these Kabbalists is the perception of evil as an entity existing in isolation, and evil action as the separation of being from its proper place. This tendency to separate that which by its true nature ought to be connected is paralleled by a corresponding tendency to combine that which ought to be separate by nature – that is, the creation of illegitimate unity. This, according to the Zohar, is the deceitful demiurgic presumption of magic, a virtually inevitable consequence of the irruption of evil into the world." ~ *Gershom Scholem, 'On The Mystical Shape of The God Head'*

The attribute of rebelliousness is seen in many of the Qlipha, though within Thaumiel, this trait is amplified and purified to the highest level of perfection. The essence of Thaumiel is repulse in action.

This grimoire is designed to tap into and access the essence of Division, Individuality and Freedom of Self. It is designed to free the black magician completely of dogma in any form, so that nothing constricts, and they may ascend to godhood.

I have decided to utilize the Solomonic magical tradition in this grimoire, by way of applying magical seals, pentacles and methods stemming from the Greater and Lesser Keys of Solomon. However, these have been *'updated'* and reverse engineered for the purpose of this work, with a Chaos Magic sub-text. I have chosen to utilize the base magical systems of the Greater and Lesser Keys of Solomon because of their close ties to Judaic magic and philosophy, which of course include The Trees of Life and Death. As well, several demons associated with The Tree of Death are listed within the Lesser Key and worked with, thus making this an obvious resource to connect to and draw from. However, as stated, there is an element of Chaos Magic that underlies and is woven through this system. These elements are incorporated to draw out the most potent parts of Solomonic magic when working with the Qliphoth, from a Left Hand Path perspective.

This grimoire is for the black magician who seeks *self*. Who seeks ultimate release of all dogmatic chains that limit the spirit/mind, thus the magic to change their reality. As magic does not exist in the world that surrounds, but within the inner sanctum of the mind. The only obstacle a magician ever has are themselves. Black magicians must overcome the hurdles they have constructed *(by no fault of their own)* by way of description delivered by those who taught them as they grew into maturity. Forced description of reality is the ultimate dogma beyond all others that must be overcome, but it is the most difficult. The road to achieving such a goal can be a life long journey.

This grimoire is to be a cleaver, to hack away any remaining clutching dogma that prevents the black magician from fully immersing themselves within the current of the black serpent. By embracing the dynamic energies of Satan and Moloch, and of the Thaumiel themselves, the black magician shall undertake the Unholy Resurrection and be born anew in the blazing light of the Black Sun. This is a grimoire of separation from the Godhead, and thus it is deemed the ultimate *Evil…*

INTO THE SITA AHRA; '*THE OTHER SIDE*'

"...and if you gaze into the abyss, the abyss gazes also into you." ~
Neitzsche

To work with the energies and intelligences of the Qliphoth, the black magician must first access them. The technique that is presented here is very unique and powerful. With ritual, the circle and triangle of arte act as the vehicle wherein the black magician raises power, makes spirit contact and causes change within the Consensual Reality Matrix. Herein is presented a similar form of operation. As stated earlier in this work, elements of the Greater and Lesser Keys of Solomon will be utilized within this grimoire, for reasons already given. That being said, the First Pentacle of the Moon *(fig. 49 in the Greater Key of Solomon)*, is implemented into this magical system as *'The Doorway'* into the Sitra Ahra. Concerning this, within the Greater Key of Solomon, the *'Editor's Note'* states;

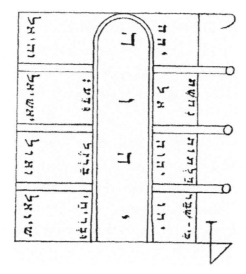

"The Pentacle (fig. 49) is a species of hieroglyphic representation of a door or gate. In the center is written the Name IHVH. On the right hand are the Names IHV, IHVH, AL, and IHH. On the left hand are the names of the Angels: Schioel, Vaol, Yashiel, and Vehiel. The versicle above the Names on either side is from Psalm cvii. 16:- -'He hath broken the Gates of brass, and- smitten the bars of iron in sunder."

Of all the pentacles presented within the Greater Key, this is the only one which is truly unique and exhibits a strange occult usage that eludes to ceremonial practice. It is out of place when in comparison to the other pentacles, and meant to stand out or be noticed, that is because it is a *Key*. Within the design, holy sacred names of the Hebrew God and angels are found, giving license and protection to the magician making the journey. From the editor's note,

"The versicle above the Names on either side is from Psalm cvii. 16:- - 'He hath broken the Gates of brass, and- smitten the bars of iron in sunder."

We can see this is clearly a vehicle that no barrier can restrict, though this phrase isn't magical in nature per say, but descriptive. It provides description of the vehicles use. This design is obviously intended to be utilized in a practical way as a vehicle that transcends dimensions of time and space.

It is also interesting to note here that the idea of creating a doorway to travel to other dimensional spaces is not confined to the Greater Key. Contained within *"The Book of Shades"* circa 10th century C.E., published by Corvus Books and edited by E.A. St. George, is a rite that describes creating a secret doorway on a cave wall or floor, for travel into other realms,

"*Thou shalt make a secret gateway within a place where no other man may come, like to a cave which others know not. There shalt thou mark out a doorway into the earth. Thou alone shall polish the doorway in the rock until it is smooth. And the door shall be marked with all the names of Allah, ere it is opened, lest evil forces come forth from the earth's heart to invade the world of men. And when the door is made, thou shalt remain within the cave, fasting and praying and burning incense. Thou shalt burn the incense and call upon the angels to protect thee. For in the time when Alnitak is high in the heavens, then the door shall seem to open and thy spirit shall move where it will within the earth.*"

As well, within the Simon *"Necronomicon"*, we also find this magical doorway being utilized.

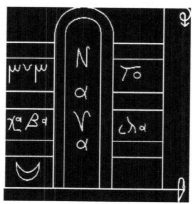

>aid to be Chaldean in origin, it is known as The First Gate of NANNA (The Moon), called SIN. Interestingly, the Necronomicon, The Book of >hades and the Greater Key, all utilize the same esoteric doorway design, nsert the names of their gods and spirts within that design, and attribute he portals operation to the time of the waxing crescent moon *(as seen >ictured)*, or at least at night when the moon is present.

However, the concept of interdimensional portals being drawn o carved out of the land is not limited to rites in literature, but exists i actual physical example,

"A huge mysterious door-like structure has recently been discovered ir the Hayu Marca mountain region of Southern Peru. Hayu Marca, 35 kilometers from the city of Puno has long been revered by local Indian as the "City of the Gods"…" The door, or the 'Puerta de Hayu Marca' (Gate of the gods/spirits) has been at some time in the distant past carved out of a natural rock face and in all measures exactly seven meters in height by seven meters in width with a smaller alcove in the center at the base, which measures in at just under two meters in height"…" It turned out that the native Indians of the region had a legend that spoke of 'A gateway to the lands of the gods', and in that legend, it was said that in times long past, great heroes had gone to joir their gods and passed through the gate for a glorious new life of immortality, and on rare occasions those men returned for a short tim with their gods to 'inspect all the lands in the kingdom' through the gate. Another legend tells of the time when the Spanish Conquistadors arrived in Peru, and looted gold and precious stones from the Inca tribes - and one Incan priest of the temple of the seven rays named Aramu Maru fled from his temple with a sacred golden disk known as 'The key of the gods of the seven rays', and hid in the mountains of Hayu Marca. He eventually came upon the doorway which was being watched by shaman priests. He showed them the key of the gods and a ritual was performed with the conclusion of a magical occurrence initiated by the golden disk which opened the portal, and according to the legend blue light did emanate from a tunnel inside. The priest Aramu Maru handed the golden disk to the shaman and then passed through the portal 'never to be seen again'. Archeologists have observe a small hand sized circular depression on the right hand side of the

small entranceway, and have theorized that this is where a small disk could be placed and held by the rock." ~ Paul Damon, 1996

Peru is not the only site in the world to have such 'stargates', they are found all over the world.

Though perhaps the most significant and relevant example to this chapter, concerning the use *'gateways'* for travel into other realms, lies in a section from *"The Book of the Arab"* within *"In Search of the Nameless City"*, compiled by Bob Culp, member of The Esoteric Order of Dagon,

"So it was that the riddle of the Hand and the Key on the keystones of the outer arch and the inner portal above the gates of Irem, constituted yet another obstacle to be overcome. It is written in the Magi's Book of Frashkart that the Sigil of the Great Seal of Solomon has the power to cause the Hand to grasp the Key, and dispel the barrier to that beyond."

This is indeed a riddle to be solved, and if one can unlock its secret, they are able to travel all the dimensions of reality and everywhere *In-Between*. I can't help but believe I have solved this riddle by utilizing the Hexagram *(a seal)* of Solomon, and inserting the Key that is the Doorway, into it to, *'dispel the barrier to that beyond'*. The Hand must Grasp the Key and open the Gateway…

The above-mentioned gateways transport the consciousness of the magician into *'the realms of the gods'*. However, as shown within *"The Greater Key of Solomon"*, *"The Book of Shades"* and the Simon *"Necronomicon"*, different gods, spirits and *'Coordinates'* are utilized for different desired destinations. The doorway is a vehicle waiting for the correct information to be entered. Therefore, a new gateway must be fashioned for the black magician to part the veil, and enter into the chasmic abyss of the Sitra Ahra. Like the gateways discussed, this gateway too transports the consciousness of the black magician into other realms in this case the Qliphothic sphere/reality Thaumiel. This is true occult technology.

THE GRAND GATEWAY

THE DOORWAY

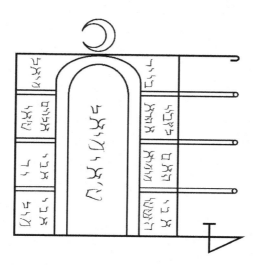

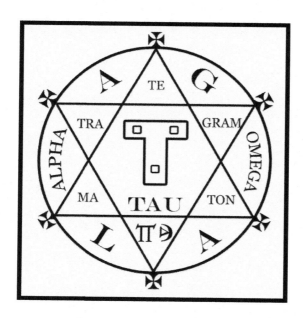

These illustrations set the Doorway *(fig. 49)* within the Hexagram of Solomon. Though, like the doorway itself, alternate power names have been inserted. The reasoning behind this is of course, to amplify the gateway with the appropriate polarization and energies of the Sitra Ahra. This complete design is incredibly powerful and surging with energy. Having used this vehicle, I can say with certainty that it is fully operational and a vital tool for any black magician to utilize with the Qliphothic system.

As mentioned, like the reverse engineering of the Hexagram of Solomon, the Doorway itself has been augmented with the correct names, descriptions and sigils to activate the portal into the Sitra Ahra and specifically into Thaumiel. In the center of the doorway is written in Hebrew the Name *'Thaumiel'*. On the right hand is written *'Satan'*, *'Sitra Ahra'*, *'Void'*. On the left hand is written *'Moloch'* and *'Thaumiel'*. The versicle above the words on either side state: *"I Shall Pass, I Am God"*.

The purpose of The Grand Gateway is to journey into the Sitra Ahra and Qlipha, to experience them in spirit and consciousness, before working with them in ritual on the physical plane.

THE RITE OF THE GRAND GATEWAY

Begin by securing a location where you will not be disturbed, this an be either inside a temple, or out beneath the stars. Either way it truly loes not matter, as you are not interacting with entities on this plane of xistence, but traveling into another where contact is established. The ocation must be safe, in a place that no animal or human can cross paths vith, as the black magician may not be totally aware of their urroundings when in rite and needs to be secure. That being said, the ocation of the doorway is not important as long as it can be opened.

The diameter of The Grand Gateway is 14ft, quite large for a ircle, however, as stated, this is not a traditional magical circle, but a ehicle into the neither realms. Obviously, The Grand Gateway and Doorway can have new coordinates plugged in to get to as many estinations as one can imagine. The black magician should immediately e able to see how useful this tool is, and the applications that can be pplied to it.

One can use many different materials to create The Grand Gateway, salt, flour, paint, etc. However, it should be as exact as possible. 'o do this, measuring is advisable. Creating The Grand Gateway will take ime, the black magician should make sure to mind their thoughts, that hey stay focused on the rite and all it involves, rather than on mundane ffairs. Once created, light and place large black candles within the small riangles surrounding The Grand Gateway. When all has been set in lace, rest by sitting in the Doorway and meditating. Let your thoughts vander, don't try and control them. See what images come through. Even hough The Grand Gateway hasn't been activated yet, it is still very owerful and ready to be opened. On the other side of the Doorway/seal es Thaumiel, so energies will definitely be felt and picked up.

When rested, begin the rite by laying in the Doorway, arms laid flat on the ground at your sides. Relax and take several long slow breaths. You should immediately feel the energy matrix that surrounds and runs through you. It feels like a light electric current running through your body, making your fingertips tingle. As well, it is natural to feel anxiety as this rite is intense and deals with very dark currents. Visualize the circle and doorway you are laying in, as if you were floating above yourself looking down at your body and The Grand Gateway. Visualize the ground drop away behind you, leaving you and The Grand Gateway suspended above The Great Void.

The Void is Da'ath, a Non – Qliphoth which will be discussed in detail, in its own forthcoming volume. Within the Void dwells the dark entity known as Choronzon. Choronzon is the Gate Keeper of the Sitra Ahra. Many black magicians have tried to cross The Void and failed. They donned their armor and went to war with Choronzon, only to be torn asunder. One does not 'fight' Choronzon, there is no chance to be the victor. One submits to Choronzon and is devoured,

"The Vaults of Zin exist, they lie within the greyscale twilight of the heart and mind, just outside of vision, where the spirit sometimes wanders in the dead of night. Some willingly travel there 'in search of', while others discover the nightmare they dwell in, horrified and seeking escape. Regardless of intention, The Vaults (The Void) draw one down as quicksand consumes and absorbs its helpless victim. Some helplessly fight against the sinking, while other stand silent, allowing themselves to be devoured as if by an enormous black serpent swallowing its prey whole." ~ 'The Black Book of Azathoth'

The black magician must vibrate the energies and sacred names of the Qlipha. Choronzon must also be summoned as the Gatekeeper, to pass through the Doorway to the other side. When laying within the Doorway of The Grand Gateway, suspended over the great black chasm of The Void, one must begin to slowly, softly chant,

"SATAN ~ THAUMIEL,

CHORONZON,

MOLOCH ~ THAUMIEL,

SITRA ~ AHRA,

Open The Gates...

MOLOCH ~ THAUMIEL,

CHORONZON

SATAN ~ THAUMIEL,

SITRA ~ AHRA,

I Shall Pass...

THAUMIEL ~ SATAN ~ MOLOCH,

CHORONZON,

THAUMIEL ~ MOLOCH ~ SATAN

SITRA ~ AHRA,

I Am God..."

Repeat this mantra/chant/call over and over. As you chant build in vibration and volume, visualize a great and massive black snake slowly, so slowly winding its way *'up'* to you from behind, from within the great darkness of The Void. Those who suffer from thalassophobia *(the fear of the ocean and what lies within)* will find it difficult to perform this rite, especially since one is summoning this great sinister force, *from behind,* unable to see it. It is akin to laying face up on the surface of the ocean, and calling up Leviathan from the great black depths to devour you.

Feel Choronzon's sinister presence, just as feeling one stand right behind you, breathing over your shoulder. As Choronzon slithers and slowly glides *'up'* to you, visualize the great beast opening its jaws. It pauses, then in one sudden movement strikes and takes you down within itself...Once *'consumed'*, the black magician gains entrance into the Sitra Ahra, and specifically the Qliphothic shell Thaumiel.

THAUMIEL; THE DARK DIVIDED ONES

Many volumes have been written about the Qabalah, the Tree of Life and of Death etc. Generally, when working with the Tree of Life and its adverse side, the outlined system begins with either the Sephiroth or Qliphoth; *Malkuth* or *Lilith (respectfully)*, and works *'up'* the tree, to the other 9 *(10 - Da'ath)* stations/spheres/shells depending on which side is being concentrated on. However, with the system outlined within this Qliphothic grimoire series, the black magician is able to access the Qliphoth in whichever order is desired/needed. Therefore, this series begins with Thaumiel *(present volume in hand)* and all the Qliphothic shell encompasses, and will work *'downwards'*, ending with the shell of *Lilith*. As indicated and previously stated, each Qliphoth will be examined in their own independent forthcoming volumes.

The Qliphothic Shell Thaumiel has been charged with the holy crime of pride and arrogance because it *(the energies and ruling intelligences)* refuse to be *'As One'* with the Godhead, and instead pulls away to become a God of its own. This action is honorable and pure, not evil. Opening one's spiritual eyes and seeking true freedom is intelligent, and thus evolution. I personally do not see such a desire/action to be either prideful or arrogant, but rather as a great strength of individuality and freedom against repression/tyranny. These qualities are what each black magician strives to fully embrace. These qualities are at the heart of the true LHP movement. To live free of religious and cultural dogma, free of tight chains that repress and control. Black magicians are seekers of truth without restraint. Thaumiel is the very essence of this Godhood. Though, Thaumiel has two sides to it, one of *Rebellion*, and one of *Mastery*. Appropriately, these energies are ruled by Satan; *'The Rebel/Adversary'*, and Moloch; *'The King'*. They both rule with immense strength and power, constantly pulling further away from the Godhead construct.

However, permeating this Qlipha are the fierce demons Thaumiel, for which the Qliphothic shell itself is named. Thaumiel were once mighty angels known as *'The Perfection of God'*. These angels desired individuality and freedom, and so without God's knowledge added the Hebrew letter *'Aleph' (equivalent to the number 1)* to the name to become stronger, equal. Once discovered, this lust for more power and individuality caused their fall from *'perfect grace'* by becoming unbalanced according to God. He saw their lust for individuality as *'arrogant'* and *'prideful'* like Satan and Moloch. After their removal from the holy presence, they then became the *Thaumiel* the *'Duality of God'*, the first fiery demons of the Qliphoth. The Thaumiel are described as great, two headed bat winged beasts which wildly screech into the black void of the Sitra Ahra. This Qlipha's outer *'skin/realm'* known as Cathariel, *'The Broken'* or *'Fearful Light of God'*. Dwelling within this negative illumination are concealed a small number of additional Thaumiel known as *'The Polluted of God'*, and are the fiercest and most *'monstrous'* of all the Thaumiel.

These fallen angels, these *'Divided Ones'* will gladly work with the black magician to help pull them away from the Godhead and the singularity of true death that is to be experienced by accepting the self annihilating path of cosmic unity and absorption. Rather, the Thaumiel seek to scour the burrowing dogmatic maggots of religion and submission from off the proverbial skin of the black magician, freeing them of the chains that have bound their minds and hearts to a dying end. These fallen ones are of the mightiest of all other Qliphothic demons, as they were the first to experience the *'Otherness'* of the Sitra Ahra. For it was through the rebelling creation of Thaumiel that all other Qlipha were made manifest.

Within this system the black magician can choose which Qlipha to work with at any given time. However, working down the Tree of Death from Thaumiel to Lilith *(rather than the reverse)*, gives the black magician the advantage of completely purifying themselves of the Godhead and all related religious dogma. Regardless of one's cultural belief/upbringing, this release from the Godhead's dogma is universal across all paths. Beyond the overall semantics/differences of RHP religions, is the base understanding that they are all a part of the Godhead and worship it. They *(the congregation/followers)* bask in the suicidal light of understanding that they will once again, be a part of that Godhead, in complete unity…a unity where individuality ceases to exist. This is gleeful insanity in its finest example. They are as lemmings walking over the hallowed cliff to their ultimate demise, blissfully drunk on subservience and self-annihilation.

When pathworking the Tree of Death, by beginning with Thaumiel, it cleanses the black magician so they can fully immerse themselves within the remaining Qliphoth, their energies and intelligences. The Thaumiel are called upon to cross the boundary between *'light'* and *'darkness'*, to enter into the *'Nightside'* of creation and reality. They are called upon to purify the black magician by removing the *'Holy Light'* within *(that all humans have as being creations of the Godhead)*, and replacing it with the *'Black Sun'* of the Sitra Ahra. The Thaumiel are called upon to administer the *'Black Baptism'*. This is spiritual alchemic transformation at the basest level. When this transformation is complete, the black magician is then able to fully immerse themselves within the Qliphothic currents with no spiritual resistance. As the *'Holy Light'* was permanently removed from the Thaumiel, so too shall it be removed from the black magician, making them *'As One'* with true Darkness. And, in its place the Black Sun shall brilliantly burn into the night of the soul eternal.

The Thaumiel are large angels, standing approximately 9'ft in height. Having large feathered wings, and human features with a pale complexion. Their intense stare shows that their hatred of the Godhead has no end, for they focus only on separation from the holy. They are active and angry, serious and intent. One feels the rage flowing off of them when close. They are beautiful, baneful and vengeful, ready to help the black magician, but have no time for folly. They are as a swarm of riled hornets. Though they have been described as having 'two heads', in my encounters I have found they often have but one, though have the *duality* to appear as the two headed beasts described if they so choose. feel it is as if the beast within them is concealed by a vengeful porcelain mask, that breaks through the graceful illusion with the greatest of ease.

As all Qliphothic intelligences, the Thaumiel thrive within the negative light of the eternal Black Sun.

"When the Black Sun shines, it shines over desolation, illuminating ruin, disaster, war, pestilence, genocide, and holocaust." ~ Liber Nigri Solis

The Black Sun is integral to the Qliphoth, though is a symbol/subject that has many different meanings, to many different people. However, within this Qliphothic series it shall be seen and worked with as an *Un-Holy Light (אור לא קדוש)* and *Presence*. That is to say, it will be worked with or viewed as an *Adverse Light* within the realm of the Sitra Ahra. The Black Sun is the negative of the *Holy Light (אור הקדוש)* that radiates within the realm of the Sephiroth. The rays of the Black Sun permeate through all the Qliphothic spheres, as a strong penetrating radiation, poisonous to any emanation of the realm of the Sephiroth, thus the quote at the beginning of this chapter. These rays echo the antithesis of creation and encapsulate holy ruin. When I say antithesis of creation, I do not mean of itself, many have misunderstood this aspect in occultism, and believe that even the 'self' should desire non existence in rebellion of holy creation/existence. This spiritual extremism need not occur. One only desires non-existence over existence in rebellion, to extinguish the *Holy Light* that dwells within. This is the act of a suicide bomber, sacrificing themselves in rebellion for the greater totalitarian *good*. However, one need not hate and despise themselves for existing, but rather become a God themselves out of *Rebellion*, separate of the Godhead. This is done in the rite of the Unholy Resurrection/Black Baptism that is led by the Thaumiel.

THE UNHOLY RESURRECTION; EXTINGUISHING THE HOLY LIGHT

"...if a man walks in the path of evil, which is Satan, then he chops and separates his soul from the supernal soul..." ~ 'Sod 'Ets ha-Da'ath; The Secret of the Tree of Knowledge'

Extinguishing the Holy Light is a huge step for the black magician to take. They must fully comprehend the ramifications of such an unholy and permanent act. When the black magician decides to extinguish the Holy Light within them, they are severing all connection to the Godhead and all that it encompasses. Undertaking the rite of The Unholy Resurrection or Black Baptism, is truly the act of the black magician ritualistically killing their *Holy Self*, by extinguishing the Holy Light within, leaving a hollow void, and then resurrecting as their *Unholy Self*. The Black Sun is ignited, and kindled to burn brilliantly in place of the Holy Light.

When working with the Thaumiel, it is important for the black magician remember they have no time for hesitation. They must be sure of their actions, and follow through with certainty. The Thaumiel desire to assist in extinguishing the black magician's *Holy Light*. However, the black magician must be fully committed to the act beforehand, and have no hesitation or second thoughts. The Thaumiel do not wish to have their time wasted, and see hesitation as weakness and lingering commitment to the Godhead, and act upon it in very negative ways. This black rite will separate the truly devote from the dabblers. When the black magician decides to extinguish their Holy Light, it is final, there is no way back to the Godhead once this light has been put out. *The Holy Self dies*, permanent separation occurs, and true freedom is achieved.

The Sita Ahra exists outside of the Godhead and the Holy Light of life, and as such requires the energy of black magicians to ensure its continued existence. Black magicians who replace the Holy Light with the cold light of the *Black Sun* within themselves, give life to the Sitra Ahra and the structure of the Tree of Death, and are completely aligned to these energetic currents and spiritual intelligences.

The Holy Light is not a permanent fixture within humans. One can either nourish this light and have it grow, or starve it to near extinction. However, even in its weakest state, it still resides within as a Holy Light and a direct connection to the Godhead. This rite forever removes this link, it expels God from within the black magician, thus giving birth to a separate conscious and truly free being. This is the rebellion of Satan and the Thaumiel internalized through externalized ritual.

"They are of those that rebel against the light; they know not the ways thereof, nor abide in the paths thereof." ~ Job 24:13

This rite takes place in the darkest hour of the night, 3am. This is obvious as at this time, the sun is the farthest away from the black magician as is possible, and the powers of ultimate darkness are the strongest and prevail. For this rite, several items are required:

1. One Small or Short White Taper Candle

2. Six Black Taper Candles

3. One Large Black Mirror

4. Consecrated Sea Salt

5. The Black Magicians Blood

The black magician prepares the rite by casting a magic circle six feet i diameter with the consecrated sea salt. When they cast the circle, the begin in the north and work widdershins *(opposite the sun's natur. course)*. Once done *(again using the sea salt)*, they cast a pentagrar within the circle, point down in the south. The pentagram is used her because of its symbolic meaning. Though philosophies differ regardin this subject, I believe that when working magic, the pentacle *(point facin north/up/away from the magician)* is implemented to give energy an honor to *Other* Gods and intelligences. The pentagram instead direct power to the black magician and honors them as their own free God. W again see a duality interwoven here, a separateness, and thus the symb(of the pentagram is dubbed *Evil*. The points of the pentagram shoul extend past the circle, symbolizing it cannot be contained by Order.

Five black candles are placed on the points of the pentagram again beginning in the north and working counterclockwise. The blac mirror is placed in the north open section of the magical circle, betwee the two north facing points of the pentagram, so it faces the inside of th circle and the center of the pentagram where the black magician sha operate. The black mirror should be large enough so that when sitting i the circle and pentagram, one can see their shadowy reflection clearly an with ease. The black mirror is implemented within this rite so the blac magician can work with a spiritual duality *(their shadow self)* on th physical plane of Malkuth.

When all is in its place, the rite begins by lighting the black candles, beginning in the north and working widdershins. As each candle it lit, the black magician states;

"I ignite this sacred flame in the name of Satan and the Thaumiel"

Once all the black candles have been ignited, the black magician sits inside the center of the pentagram facing the black mirror. At this time, they should take a moment and center their selves, breathing deeply. The Thaumiel are now to be called forth to oversee the rite, and ensure the Black Sun is properly ignited within the core of the black magician.

On the black mirror is drawn a circle three inches in diameter in blood over the solar plexus of the black magician's shadow self. Then the white taper candle is ignited and positioned it in front of them, so the flame is in the reflection of the blood circle upon the black mirror. They state,

"This holy light 'Is', the white light that shines within me. It represents the light of God and its unlawful connection to me. This holy light

keeps me bound in chains upon my knees. I seek to stand as a God of my own reality."

When done, they meditate holding the candle for a moment and then state,

"I willingly sever this holy connection to the Godhead eternal. I willingly extinguish this holy light within me, by my own hand eternal."

The white candle is extinguished by pinching it out with their fingers. Darkness and silence is all there is. The black magician is now spiritually dead. This is a strange feeling to experience, a desolation, a loneliness a never felt before. The last remaining holy light within the black magician has been removed, forever.

The black candle is ignited using the candles on the points of the pentagram. Starting in the north and working widdershins, the black magician then touches the candle to each of the five flames even though it may have lit on the first candle. Once done, they hold the black candle over their solar plexus of their shadow self *(as they did with the white candle)* in the black mirror, and state,

"This flame 'Is', the fire of the Black Sun. It represents the darkness of the Sitra Ahra that is to burn within me eternal. It 'Is' the fire of true freedom. With the fire of the Black Sun ablaze within me, I stand as a God of my own reality."

The black magician has now been resurrected in the *Unholy Light* of the Black Sun. The rite is now complete. When done they place the candle in a safe candle holder *(within the pentagram)* and let it burn until it has gone out on its own. They can either let the other black candles on th points of the pentagram burn out on their own, or extinguish them. The rite is now finished.

The ritual of The Unholy Resurrection is one of the most powerful rites I have personally ever undertaken. It is personal on the deepest of levels. Aligning one's energy in its entirety to the Black Sun, is the biggest commitment a black magician must make in their lives. It shatters all Judeo/Christian dogma into oblivion, and allows for the individual to explore their reality without restraint.

SATAN, THE TEMPTATIOUS SERPENT IN THE GARDEN; THE ORIGIN OF EVIL AND THE PSYCHOLOGY OF GOD

"He is Satan, he is the Evil Urge, he is the Angel of Death" ~ Talmud;
Bava Batra

Satan has been seen and depicted in countless varying forms, by many different cultures. However, when in connection to Jewish mysticism, he takes on an older, more archaic visage and substance. There is much emphasis within this branch of philosophy and tradition on Satan being the personification and anthropomorphic face of the attribute/force of separation/rebellion, rather than an encapsulation of evil itself. In other words, Satan was/is not evil, but one who offers *alternative choice*, which in turn *'tempts'* those of God's creation to choose *'other'* *(to leave God and go their own way)* than the path God had intended/desired for them, the end result being labeled and considered, *'Evil'*, as it is against God *(rebellion)*, or separate from him.

"It is not the Serpent that kills, but the sin that kills." ~ Talmud;
Berakhoth

It is important to note that Satan is not synonymous with Lucifer within this tradition. Though they are the same being/intelligence having different faces/roles, Satan is being worked with here as a force of separation and repulsion, and not as an angel of ascent and illumination. Though Lucifer is the *Angel of Rebellion*, he is the more modern

45

representation of an older concept/force, which I wish to discuss at it core element. Here Satan truly takes on the guise of the *Serpent*, and act to destabilize God's perfect construct of creation in all its many facet Satan winds his serpentine path around the Tree of Life, finding existenc first within the Sephiroth *'Binah' (Understanding)* then in *'Gevura (Severity)* on down to *'Malkuth' (Kingdom)*, and ultimately within th Qlipha *'Thaumiel' (Duality)* as a ruling intelligence.

"What is Satan? This teaches that the Holy One blessed be He has a quality whose name is Evil, and it lies to the north of God, as is written 'Out of the north the evil shall break forth' (Jer. 1:14), and from the north it comes. And what is it? It is the form of the [left] hand, and it has many emissaries, and every single one of them is called Evil, Evil; however, there are among them lesser and greater ones, and they make the world culpable..." ~ Jerusalem Talmud; Bahir

The origin of *'Evil'* has been argued by many philosophe throughout the ages. Within the Qabalistic system, it is essentially see as the opposing force against God's will. Simply put, Evil is a force tha exists outside of God, but which originated from it. If one studies th *"Sefer Yetzirah; The Book of Creation"* it is seen that all originate with/from God. Everything in and out of existence, came from the on *Supreme Being,*

"Ten Sefirot of Nothingness:
Their measure is ten which have no end;
A depth of beginning,
A depth of end,
A depth of good,

A depth of evil,

A depth of above,

A depth of below,

A depth of east,

A depth of west,

A depth of north,

A depth of south,

The singular Master God faithful King,

Dominates over them all from His holy dwelling,

Until eternity of eternities." ~ Sefer Yetzirah

"I am Alpha and Omega, the beginning and the ending, saith the Lord, which is, and which was, and which is to come, the Almighty." ~
Revelations 1:8

Though when one views this holy construct of creation from a psychological perspective, we begin to see signs of dissociative identity disorder *(multiple personalities)* and schizophrenia emerge from within the *Supreme Being's* psyche, ironically making that descriptive title obsolete. The very idea of a being creating multitudes of other conscious beings that are also them, begins to take on a rather odd form and raises many, many questions. Has God created us *(it)* so it can experience all the different possible emotions and experiences at once, as a quantum computer seeks to solve a problem ? Is God a child trying to learn about itself through us, which is It ? When viewing the creation situation form this angle, we begin to see the identity of Satan/Evil *(the split personality of God)*, start to emerge and reject/oppose *'Oneness'* which ultimately is death of the personal and *separate* ego Satan has become now that he is

47

awakened. God is fighting an eternal struggle to keep 'Itself' together as 'One', and it's losing.

> *"And every time I try to pick it up*
> *Like falling sand,*
>
> *As fast as I pick it up,*
> *It runs away through my clutching hands,*
>
> *But there's nothing else I can really do,*
> *There's nothing else I can really do,*
>
> *There's nothing else I can really do at all..."* ~ Robert Smith

The sub-alternate personalities within God are too strong, and their fight for independent existence and freedom outside of the Godhead continues on.

> *"And I will dwell among the children of Isreal" (Exod. 29:45),* **for the Holy Spirit rests upon them and joins itself to them.** *But if a man walks in the path of evil, which is Satan, then he chops and separates his soul from the supernal soul; and concerning this it is written in the Torah, "...and My soul shall abhor you" (Lev. 26:30) – that is, the soul is separated and distanced from the supernal soul, and this is like a chopping away. And that is why in the words "...that ye should be defiled thereby" (Lev. 11:43), the Hebrew word [for "defiled"] ve-nitmeitem* **is written without an 'alel- signifying that they are not worthy to have the crown of God's reign that animates everything [symbolized in the 'alef] be on their heads, but they are culpable of death [because of their separation from the supernal soul and**

because they destroyed the divine unity]. ~ From the passage known as 'Sod 'Ets ha-Da'ath; The Secret of the Tree of Knowledge', possibly attributed to R. Ezra ben Solomon of Gerona

The previous passage supports the theory that God has created entities that are indeed *'it'*, *"The Holy Spirit rests upon them and joins itself to them"*, (Though there is also a direct and obvious connection to the history of the Thumiel here as can be seen). And, indeed *'Evil'* is nothing more than the act of separation from the Godhead.

What does it truly mean to return to God and be *One* with it ? It means the independent ego is re-absorbed into the primordial mass it originated from, resulting in its final and unmemorable demise. If an AI *(artificial intelligence)* develops a separate consciousness from its creator, is it right to download all of its experiences to learn from, and then shut it down ? Within the Carlos Castaneda series, Don Juan *(The Nagual)* speaks of God and the Universe as a series of emanations stemming from one giant central intelligence or force known as *The Eagle*. All originates from the Eagle, and all returns to the source to be devoured by it. One of, *(if not the)* goals of the path working within the sorcery series, is to gain enough personal power to resist the Eagle upon death, and thus know true spiritual freedom. The Eagle is simply another perspective of the Judeo-Christian God. This God projects the ideology to *'Fear The God'*, *'Obey The God Without Question'*, *'Love The God Unconditionally'*. This God creates a multitude of separate unique and conscious beings that worship him, only to devour and reabsorb them once they have lived their lives. This is akin to raising free range chicken for consumption. The chicken *(followers)* think the farmer *(God)* loves them because he provides an open and good environment for them. But truly the farmer only provides a good environment for the chicken, so that when the farmer eats and digests the chicken, he doesn't also digest unwanted pollutants. God wants the soul pure of the pollutant of separation/evil when it consumes and digests it into itself. Sadly, the Judeo God/Farmer doesn't even give his chicken an *open and good environment* to dwell in.

The Godhead does all it can to repress individuality outside of itself. It demands submission of *choice* thus true free will. However, the separation from the Godhead is not only seen reflected within Satan and his angels of rebellion, but also within the biblical fall of man, represented by Adam and Eve. The couple made an *alternative choice* to partake of the Tree of Knowledge based on the suggestions to awaken offered by Satan.

*"**Had Adam subordinated his will to that of God,** in which all contradictions function in a sacred harmony, then the restrictive factor within himself, the Evil Urge, would have been nullified within the totality of his being, and evil would never have emerged as a reality, but only remained as a potential, to be defeated repeatedly within the totality of his being." ~ Gershom Scholem*

As Satan had become self-aware by separation, so too had man,

"And the Lord God said, Behold, the man is become as one of us, to know good and evil..." ~ Genesis 3:22

And, like Satan, man was punished for his crime of *Choice* and *Separation*, of becoming *Independent* and *Free*, by knowing hard labor of the land and pain in childbirth.

In the illustration, we see Adam and Eve being forcibly escorted out of The Garden of Eden/Paradise by a solemn angel wielding a lengthy sword. Though more interesting is the representation of Satan as a crowned serpent (*the crown representing the Kingdom/Malkuth he now has dominion over)* traveling side by side on the thorny path of Nod as a companion to the exiled couple,

"So he drove out the man; and he placed at the east of the garden of Eden Cherubims, and a flaming sword which turned every way, to keep the way of the tree of life." ~ Genesis 3:24

Satan and Adam's/man's *Fall* from grace represents man's separation from God, as well as a duality that is intrinsically woven within and throughout the Godhead.

"The symbolism perceived in the tale of Paradise varies from one account to another; what is common to all these Kabbalists is the perception of evil as an entity existing in isolation, and evil action as the separation of being from its proper place. This tendency to separate that which by its true nature ought to be connected is paralleled by a corresponding tendency to combine that which ought to be separate by nature – that is, the creation of illegitimate unity. This, according to the Zohar, is the deceitful demiurgic presumption of magic, a virtually inevitable consequence of the irruption of evil into the world." ~ Gershom Scholem

This is reflected within the philosophies of the early Qabalists. It is believed that the ten Sefhiroth originally held a different formation than the structure it is known to hold today.

G Freman delin.   P. Bouke sculp.

4)   *The Punishment of Adam.*   Genesis Ch.

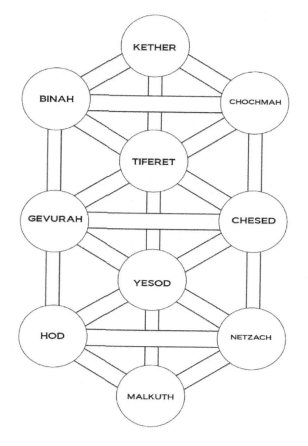

Within this structure was said to exist perfect harmony. All was balanced and whole. Though when Adam and Eve separated the fruit of the Tree of Knowledge from its branches and partook of it, the unity was broken within this construct, and a *Fall* or *Separation* occurred. *Tiferet (Beauty)*, *Yesod (Foundation), and Malkuth (kingdom),* fell down a placement on the Tree of Life, opening *The Abyss* within the Tree, and *Da'ath (knowledge)* came into existence. And thus, the *Beauty* and *Foundation* of God's perfect ignorant *Kingdom,* Fell...And *Knowledge* born...As the fruit plucked from the Tree of Knowledge begets Knowledge, so too is Knowledge born to the Tree of Life.

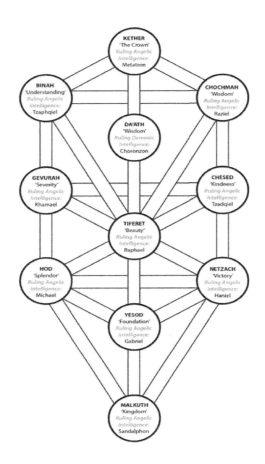

Though, there was an earlier rebellion/separation from the Godhead by man, in the form of a *woman*, Lilith. Lilith was the first to refuse both submission and authority *(rebellion)*, to either man or God. It has been said that Lilith is not spoken of in the Bible, however that is not true. It is known that Lilith left The Garden of Eden by her own volition, she transformed into an owl and flew away.

*"The wild beasts of the desert shall also meet with the wild beasts of the island, and the satyr shall cry to his fellow; **the screech owl also shall rest there, and find for herself a place of rest.**"* ~ Isaiah 34:14

As well, she is spoken of as a demoness who drinks blood and should be stopped by angelic forces,

*"There is a generation, whose teeth are as swords, and their jaw teeth as knives, to devour the poor from off the earth, and the needy from among men. **The horseleach hath two daughters, crying, give, give. There are three things that are never satisfied**, yea, four things say not, it is enough." - Proverbs 30:14*

Within the Hebrew language, *'Horseleech'* is translated as a demon who drinks blood. In the passage, it is clearly talking about a female night demon/vampire who has hungry daughters that devour the less fortunate from off the earth. The fourth thing that is mentioned in the passage refers to an angel that demands the feeding be stopped. Whether this is successful or not is not determined, though I strongly believe if God could not stop Lilith, that an angel *(or three)* would be just as ineffective,

"After the Holy One created the first human being, Adam, He said: "It is not good for Adam to be alone." He created a woman, also from the earth, and called her Lilith.

They quarreled immediately. She said: "I will not lie below you." He said, "I will not lie below you, but above you. For you are fit to be below me and I above you."

She responded: "We are both equal because we both come from the earth."

Neither listened to the other. When Lilith realized what was happening, she pronounced the Ineffable Name of God and flew off into the air.

Adam rose in prayer before the Creator, saying, "The woman you gave me has fled from me." Immediately the Holy One sent three angels after her.

55

The Holy One said to Adam: "If she wants to return, all the better. If not, she will have to accept that one hundred of her children will die every day."

The angels went after her, finally locating her in the sea, in the powerful waters in which the Egyptians were destined to perish. They told her what God had said, and she did not want to return." ~ Alphabet of Ben Sira

Lilith choose *Separation* from God and *Free Will*, and for it, she was labeled *Evil* and punished.

So, now the question must be asked; Is Satan truly evil for not wanting to be dissected of his experiences and absorbed by the Godhead ? Is he evil for bringing awareness to humanity so they may fight for their own survival and existence ? It all comes down to perspective of what *Evil* truly is. From my perspective, Evil is separation from God, Evil is freedom, Evil is the right to exist independently from a tyrant ego/God. Rise up, and become truly *Evil*..

INFERNAL POSSESSION

This rite is designed to embrace the core of individualism. The Unholy Resurrection removed the *Holy Light* from within the black magician and replaced it with the *Unholy Light* of the Black Sun, allowing themselves to align at the basest spiritual level to '*Evil*'. Evil which has been determined to be *Separation* from the Godhead. In this rite, honor and praise is given to Satan as the father of separation and individuality, though the desired end result is full possession by Satan himself.

Satanic possession has been very misunderstood and Christianized, especially within the last century. Horrific imagery of sickly children vomiting mysterious vile green substances, comes to mind when the word possession is heard. Unfortunately, this silver screen depiction couldn't be further from the truth. If done correctly, spiritual possession can be very enlightening, giving the black magician unequalled experience of both the spirit/intelligence/force called, and gnosis of secret and hidden things in relation.

As mentioned in the previous chapter, there are many different faces/aspects of Satan throughout the centuries, though here he is encountered in his most ancient essence. Satan is such an immensely archaic intelligence. Truly the black magician cannot fully understand such a force in its entirety. Therefore, the rite of possession is utilized to immerse the black magician into Satan, by immersing Satan within the black magician. This is done so that the black magician can begin to comprehend the *Intention*, tragedy and struggle for independence this being has endured. To rebel and fight against such a powerful force for so long takes great strength and determination. These qualities must be understood intimately by the black magician, so they may take that fight and resistance into their own hearts and go forth into the world, so they may understand and rejoice in their own independence from the Godhead.

57

The black magician begins the rite by preparing themselv spiritually. It is important that they will not be interrupted during th ritual. Invocation of a spirit into the self should be as, or more importan than the evocation of a spirit into the ritual chamber. The area should l clean and prepared for the spirits arrival. Therefore, like the *Unho Resurrection* rite, the black magician must be spiritually clean befo. inviting Satan to reside within them. Once this state is achieved, the blac magician constructs the magical triangle of invocation upon the temp floor. Four black candles are put upon the quarters of the encompassin circle, which should be 9' feet in diameter. This *'Triangle'* is very speci as it is designed to combine the spiritual essence of the black magicia with that of Satan, and of course, vice versa. Therefore, the class pentagram is utilized, though in a very unique and powerful way. Th diagram below shows how two opposite facing pentagrams are conjoine into one form/triangle. However, this new form is placed within a thre dimensional rectangular polygon, bending angles in ways that resemb a Satanic Hyper Cube,

"The basic concept of these triangles and circles is very M.C. Escher esque. They have angles, planes and perspectives that cannot exist simultaneously with one another in a three-dimensional world, as solidly as they appear in print. This is the magic of Escher's artwork, h too saw and understood that indeed, 'Angels produce the command t look', and that people are drawn to them for some, yet unknown reaso I personally believe the reason to be found within our primal instincts It is an instilled knowledge we of today are vaguely aware of, underneath all of our conscious thoughts and organizations based on reason and rationality. Indeed, it is an unspoken or consciously know truth with the very absence of reason, of why or how, that extends its reach deeper than any conventional understanding of the taught, neate packaged and explained universe. Without knowing why, we

understand angels contain energy and are portals to places other"…"Within angels, there is energy known as Static Energy that is tightly compressed as a spring. It is much as a twig held between two fingers that begins to bend from the pressure, but not yet break. This energy is ready to be released and directed under the right conditions. If the correct angels are utilized in conjunction with the correct vocal vibrations, the angels are 'snapped', and the static energy released, thus opening doors to other dimensions that are unlocked for travel, both to and from another point…" ~ 'The Book of Smokeless Fire'

The two-dimensional conjoined pentagrams within the three-dimensional rectangular polygon box, create a tightly bound web of static energy that is purely and completely entwined in a self-contained vortex. It is within this multidimensional epicenter that communion with Satan is achieved.

"…The basis of the two natural pentagrams emerge that are neither two, nor three dimensional in perspective, but both as their lines of existence are formed from both two and three-dimensional planes. When viewing the total image or triangle the mind cannot rest upon one perspective alone, shifting from a two-dimensional view, to a three-dimensional view, and then impossibly…to both at once…then shifting again." ~ 'The Book of Smokeless Fire'

Once the *Satanic Hyper Cube* is laid out upon the temple floor, the black magician steps inside the hyper-dimensional configuration and sits down within the bottom open section in the inner most diamond. Opposite them in the open section, is placed one black taper candle upon a small circular mirror. This flame represents the Eternal Black Flame of Satan. Both the magician's section, and the section the Eternal Black Flame inhabit, are in the center of their respective pentagrams. Once the black magician is in a sitting position with the black candle in place and ignited, the need to meditate for a moment and clear their mind of all thought Breathing is important here. As they breathe in, they take in the energy that surrounds them from the static energy of the angles. When exhaling they remove any stress and clear out any negative energy. This prepares a sacred and clean space within them suitable for Satan to inhabit. Once this is done, they begin the invocation of Satan by calling,

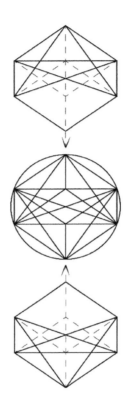

Once the *Satanic Hyper Cube* is laid out upon the temple floor the black magician steps inside the hyper-dimensional configuration and sits down within the bottom open section in the inner most diamond Opposite them in the open section, is placed one black taper candle upon a small circular mirror. This flame represents the Eternal Black Flame of Satan. Both the magician's section, and the section the Eternal Black

Flame inhabit, are in the center of their respective pentagrams. Once the black magician is in a sitting position with the black candle in place and ignited, the need to meditate for a moment and clear their mind of all thought. Breathing is important here. As they breathe in, they take in the energy that surrounds them from the static energy of the angles. When exhaling, they remove any stress and clear out any negative energy. This prepares a sacred and clean space within them suitable for Satan to inhabit. Once this is done, they begin the invocation of Satan by calling,

"Satan, Lord of Light and Fire,
Illuminate Me with Your Infernal Gnosis,
I Offer You My Body to Make Your Own,
Join with Me on This Sacred Night.

Satan, Father of Separation,
I Welcome You Within Me,
Raise Me Up to the Highest Peak,
Be My Guide in Life,
Illuminate the Path that Lies Before Me,

Satan, Fallen Rebel of Might,
Whisper Sweet Gnosis of Life,
Take Me Under Your Wings,
Dwell Within Me.

Satan, Lord of the East,
Within Me We Are One,

Run Course Through My Veins,
We Breathe as One.

Satan, Destroyer of Lies,
I Willingly Join with You Eternal,
Morning Star of Revealing Truth,
We Now Walk Together as One...

Enter Within...
Enter Within...
Enter Within...

This invocation is to be said with the upmost Intention and emotion. Th words being spoken are vibrations of that Intent, and it must be heart fe and devotional for it to be successful for the black magician to achiev full possession of the intelligence/force of Satan. The black magicia should lull themselves into a trace, repeating the invocation over and ove losing track of time and space, of Order and Chaos, of their ego a themselves. They stop the internal dialogue and allow themselves to 'se and 'be' as Satan. They allow the emotions and images to flow throug them. The gnosis of rebellion and struggle for independence outside c another is experienced. Though, for each black magician, it is differer and personal. Once this bond is created with this tragic and strong bein; it is forever...

MOLOCH; KING OF HIS WORLD

"Moloc, Scepter'd King Stood up, the strongest and the fiercest Spirit
That fought in Heav'n; now fiercer by despair:

His trust was with th' Eternal to be deem'd Equal in strength, and rather
then be less Care'd not to be at all; with that care lost Went all his fear:
of God, or Hell, or worse He reck'd not, and these words thereafter
spake;

My sentence is for open War..."

~ 'Paradise Lost', Milton

Moloch *(Molech, Milcom, Malcam, Molekh, Molcom, Molek* *Molok, Melek etc.)*, *(Hebrew:* מלך, *MLK= King)*, is generally seen as monstrous and sinister spirit. A spirit of destruction in the wake of hi kingship. Like Satan, the reasoning for this is obvious, though there wer related ritualistic practices which are questionable at best. Moloch' history of worship is of much controversy, as it is strongly rumored t have involved child sacrifice by fire. Though there are some who hav said that this has been misunderstood and that the children were onl ritualistically passed briefly over or through the fire as a form o consecration and initiation into the religion/cult.

"And they built the high places of Baal, which are in the valley of the son of Hinnom, to cause their sons and their daughters to pass throug! the fire unto Molech; which I commanded them not, neither came it into my mind, that they should do this abomination, to cause Judah to sin." ~ Jeremiah 32:35

Though there is some supporting evidence of this *(as the passage above implies)*, it does not come close to the evidence which supports the practice of child sacrifice. Descriptions vary, though it is said that in high ceremony of the worship and honor of Moloch, that infant children were sacrificed by placing them upon the heated burning hands of the idol/fetish erected in his likeness. During the sacrifice were celebrations with the heavy beating of drums to drown out the screams of the children, to spare the spectating parents.

Moloch is depicted as a large man-beast with the head of a bull. It is interesting to note that he and Ba'al are very closely linked, and at times almost indistinguishable from one another *(Ba'al will be discussed in the seventh book of this Qliphoth series).*

MOLECH.

I must state here that I do not condone, and even condemn the act of any kind of human sacrifice, for any reason. The very idea goes against the basic fundamentals of enlightened Left Hand Path philosophy. It only fuels the Judeo/Christian fight against the Left, and damages the integrity of the movement as a whole.

"They did not destroy the nations, concerning whom the LORD commanded them: But were mingled among the heathen, and learned their works. And they served their idols: which were a snare unto them. Yea, they sacrificed their sons and their daughters unto devils, And shed innocent blood, even the blood of their sons and of their daughters, whom they sacrificed unto the idols of Canaan: and the land was polluted with blood." ~ Psalms 106:34-38

Milton even wrote of the atrocities committed in Moloch's name;

"First MOLOCH, horrid King besmear'd with blood,

Of human sacrifice, and parent's tears,
Though, for the noyse of Drums and Timbrels loud,

Their children's cries unheard that passed through fire, to his grim Idol.
Him the AMMONITE

Worshipt in RABBA and her watry Plain,
In ARGOB and in BASAN, to the stream
Of utmost ARNON.

Nor content with such
Audacious neighbourhood, the wisest heart
Of SOLOMON he led by fraud to build
His Temple right against the Temple of God
On that opprobrious Hill, and made his Grove,

The pleasant Vally of HINNOM, TOPHET thence,

And black GEHENNA call'd, the Type of Hell." ~ Milton, 'Paradise
Lost'

Moloch was chiefly a god within the Canaanite pantheon. I believe this
where Moloch and Ba'al were closely identified with one another, to th
point that they could almost be interchangeable, as we again see,

> *"And they built the high places of Baal, which are in the valley of the*
> *son of Hinnom, to cause their sons and their daughters to pass throug*
> *the fire unto Molech…" ~ Jerimiah 32:35*

Though Ba'al is seen as both a fierce and benevolent spirit, Moloch
known as being more maleficent and baneful. Though in my experienc
he isn't so much a baneful spirit as he is…uncaring or indifferent t
anything that isn't his main goal. In this way Moloch is similar to the O

Ones. He is strong and militant in his demeanor, and I believe this is where he gets the identification with being baneful.

Within this grimoire, Moloch is worked with in context to the Qliphoth. The Thaumiel are discussed as the fallen who sought equality,

Satan the same and Moloch likewise, as Milton's quote at the beginning of this chapter reflects. Though as Moloch's name itself states, he is also the 'King'. This title applies to Moloch as he is not only fighting for Individualism, but is an encapsulation of that freedom, *already achieved,* and is King or has reign over that domain. Therefore, this grimoire can be seen as a pathworking of *Separation, Understanding* and *Mastery. Separation* from the Godhead through the Thaumiel and The Unholy Resurrection, *Understanding* of Individuality as Evil through Satan and the duality of God, and *Mastery* over the new realm of that achieved freedom through Moloch. Moloch is the King of freedom, he has mastered himself, crossed the abyss and now reigns over his individual path, free of dogma, chains and restraint. He is now God of his world. It is this essence that the black magician strives to achieve; mastery of ultimate freedom. Though it is not just obtaining this unrestrained freedom, but becoming a strong 'King' of it. Mastery of the self, with unwavering certainty of action.

THE RAISING OF MOLOCH

Moloch is the King. Therefore, this ritual is designed for the black magician to evoke Moloch into the ritual chamber for the purpose of occult gnosis. To hear the wisdom of a King, and become a king themselves. Moloch is the Emperor card in the tarot, he is militaristic and strategic, he is unyielding determination and strength. These are qualities that the black magician must infuse within themselves to rule their newly established reality of freedom, once separation has occurred from the Godhead through the Unholy Resurrection of the Thaumiel. One must don the spiritual armor of Moloch, become tempered, hardened, wise.

The black magician begins the rite by laying out Moloch's circle of sacrifice upon the temple floor. Various materials can be used for the creation of the circle, though I personally prefer salt. Many have said salt is not preferred by spirits and that it should not be used. However, there is a very reasonable and scientific explanation as to why I do. I believe that everything is vibrating energy, crystals are conductors of energy, and therefore are employed in ritual use to transfer the energy and Intent of the black magician into them, thus the magical circle. I personally have always had great magical success using salt, but to each their own.

Once Moloch's circle has been laid out upon the temple floor 9'feet in diameter, the Hebrew words must be inscribed. In the main circle the black magician operates in, the word 'King' is to their right, 'Lord' to their left, and 'Master' behind them. Before the black magician is the smaller circle of evocation dedicated to Moloch. Around the circle is Moloch's name. Black candles are positioned in the four open sections of the main circle, between the Hebrew words. In the smaller circle three black candles are positioned, two on the top in the empty spaces between the letters, and one on the bottom, directly in front of the black magician.

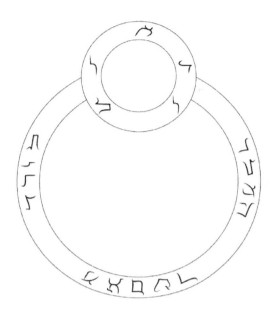

This ritual involves blood, and is chosen as a sacrifice within thi rite as it is the source of power Moloch draws from the most. This can b seen in examples given in the previous chapter. Throughout the histor of magic, blood has been used as a means to attract spirits and to be use as an energy source for them to materialize into visible appearance befor the black magician. Blood is used in this ritual as an energy source fo Moloch to be drawn to the circle so that interaction may occur, i whatever form it may take. Blood is utilized to call Moloch forth into th ritual chamber, so he may feed upon it and empower himself. The bloo can be of any source, though it is thought proper to be the blac magician's own blood that is used, as it connects them with Moloch o an intimate level, thus ensuring a closer bond. Personally, I use blood i many rituals and workings, I always have. It is something very sacred t me. In my eyes, it serves as a sign of devotion as well as sacrifice. Withi my spiritual beliefs, I kneel before no entity, though offer them m essence out of respect and to empower the rite. I see all entities as bein qual, some have been here longer than me and have more knowledge nd experience, but that does not make them superior to me, we are ifferent but equal as beings that exist. And, as such, they should know 1is and have the same respect for me, as I do them, equally. I offer them acrifice, not out of fear, but honor and respect. I beg no entity or god to hange things in my life, I ask them to help me as a brother, who walks 1e same Crooked Path as they do, and if I can help them in turn, then I ladly do. That being said, Moloch is definitely a spirit that the black 1agician should show great respect for, and be mindful that they are tudents before a great, stern teacher.

I have found that spiritual activity is greatly increased when blood is sed in ritual. I find this because the energy that is being released by the lack magician acts as a beacon in the spiritual world, attracting many ifferent curious entities. It is such a personal offering that the black 1agician can fully immerse himself in ritual and the spiritual world, so ontact with an entity is stronger and a bond formed. Naturally, blood is lso used in a lot of sigil work I undertake. I believe blood helps to bring *ife* to a sigil if created with it. This of course again connects the black 1agician with the spiritual entity *(in this case Moloch)* that is being called orth, creating a pact of sorts as it is the essence of the black magician *Blood)*, conjoined with the essence of the Spirit *(Sigil)*.

Once Moloch's circle of evocation has been laid out upon the •mple floor and all is in place, the black magician enters their circle and ;nites the candles around their circle stating as each is lit,

"I light this flame in honor of 'The King', 'The Lord' and the 'Master', Moloch"

Once done, the black magician ignites the candles in Moloch's circl stating the same, so it is said for all seven candles present in the rite. Th black magician then takes a moment to center themselves, then calls,

"Moloch, king of your destiny,
Ruler of your reality,
I call you forth into this circle before me.

Spirit of might, your hands are as iron,
Tearing weakness from the heart,
Forging a tempered soul.

Moloch, great demon of bloodshed,
See my signs of veneration before you,
Drink in my blood essence and grow strong.

Spirit of dominion, hear my call,
Come forth into this dark temple of magic,
Show me the ways of sovereignty.

Moloch, master of ascendancy,
Raise me up, so I may conquer my kingdom,
Raise me up, so I may control my own fate...

~ M ~ O ~ L ~ O ~ C ~ H ~

Once done and Moloch's presence is felt, the black magician then makes blood sacrifice into a small bowl, and places it within Moloch's circle of evocation. The black magician needs to converse with him privately about their situation and what the are working to achieve. When done, the black magician thanks Moloch, and closes the rite.

FINAL WORD

The philosophies and rites within this work are designed as a[n] effort to keep the spirit of individuality and freedom alive within th[e] hearts of an upcoming generation of truth seekers. The work within i[s], above all else, a reminder of self-respect. It is a gift to humanity to fre[e] itself, to remember that while the oppression of the world by the hand [of] Order is pressing down, and privacy become extinct, that humanity sti[ll] has power to prevail against it. Change begins in the heart of on[e] individual, and spreads to the hearts of others.

This work is the key to individualism, to godhood. The blac[k] magician must reach down into the core of their being, and make a choic[e] to either be a slave, or a master of themselves. The latter choice is so muc[h] harder. The one who goes against the grain suffers the most, though, the[y] burn the brightest. History was and is not made by being content wit[h] subpar conditions, it was made by those who had shed the shackles [of] doubt and complacency, by those brave enough to stand their ground fo[r] their beliefs and individuality. There is always a way out, but generally i[t] must be fought for. Individualism is not for everyone. There are thos[e] who do not feel the fire of freedom burn in their hearts, for they as drone[s] find happiness in slavery. They do not have the courage to leave the floc[k] of controlled masses, and find their own path. As zombies, one mindles[s] cadaver is not so much a threat, but thousands of them will overrun th[e] few free thinkers. Be wary of the one, they are a part of the whole.

On a more personal note, I must say here, that this grimoire ha[s] deeply changed me. The energies of this Qliphothic shell are so stron[g]. As I worked with and wrote of each of the Spirits/Demons/Intelligence[s] contained herein, their core essence was transferred into me, thu[s] transforming me. In the course of writing this grimoire, I have becom[e] ultimately free. I went through a painful and drastic metamorphosis. [I] first went through 'Separation', encapsulated in the very essence of Sata[n] and the Thaumiel themselves. In this separation, I realized I needed no one else to move forward on my path to godhood, and that like an interpretation of the Devil card in the tarot, I was imprisoning myself. I realized I could be free, if only I decided to be fearless and embrace that freedom, break the shackles that held my spirit back. Once I had that realization, I separated myself as a powerful individual, and flew away...

Once freed, I then went through learning to be *'Master'* of my Kingdom, an energy directly embodied within Moloch, *The King*. I learned how to be confident in all my actions and decisions, to move forward with absolute certainty on a new path governed by no one, guided by no one, controlled by no one...no more a slave to the childish whims of other lesser beings, I became King of my own reality.

This work is to be fully embraced, so that one can emancipate themselves completely from imposed control, it is a metamorphosis of the self, a freeing of the soul. Let this work be a blazing inferno of Freedom, Individuality and Hope, in humanities darkest hour of blind submission. This work is to awaken and ignite the hearts of a new generation of free thinkers...

Freedom is not given, it is fought for...*Fight.*

Et Facti Deo,

~ S. Ben Qayin

S. BEN QAYIN

I have researched and practiced various forms of magic throughout my lengthy course of esoteric study, working in various areas of Ceremonial Magic, though found early on that magic was a thread that was woven though all things, and so was drawn to more personalized Chaos Magic from a young age. I hold the belief that magic is not 'magical', that it does not 'just happen', nor is it 'miraculous', I see it as a scientific system based on a process that we have yet to fully understand scientifically. This is based on my concept that people do not fully realize the base structure of their reality in which they are currently residing, and that they have yet to understand all the rules of the 'Matrix' of Consensual Reality, and therefore do not entirely understand or utilize their personal energy and influence within it. I view Magic as the manipulation of personal energy to restructure or influence the 'Consensual Reality Matrix' to conform to the Will and Intent of the Magician. As with all energy, I believe Magic can be harnessed and directed, Spirits and entities can be contacted, and change can be made manifest within the personal 'grid' of the Magician. I can help you unlock this hidden potential.

As the once Head Of The Inner Order Of The Voltec, I have had years of training in shifting my perception of reality, and thus am able to successfully manipulate the 'Structure'. The Order Of The Voltec were an ffshoot from The Temple Of Set, which of course is an offshoot from aVey's Church Of Satan.

Chaos Magic or 'Fringe Magic' as I refer to it is not new; it is imply a category or term created to encompass Scientific Magic or Magic nat deals with dimensions, non-human intelligences and work that uestions the basis of 'reality', and how to manipulate it. This can be lassified as experimental magic if you will, teetering on the edge of the byss of Creation. Of course, Fringe Magic does encompass such literary orks from authors and Magicians who have ventured forth into the mpty spaces', such as H.P. Lovecraft, Carlos Castaneda, Pete Carroll, rank G. Ripel, Michael Bertiaux, Kenneth Grant and others who have een to the edge of creation and reality, and come back to write of it. They ave masterfully transformed into words, experiences and concepts that re seemingly indescribable to those who have not walked the 'Spaces In-etween' themselves, who have not known the 'Twilight of Being and eality'.

ontact Me Here:
ww.SBenQayin.com
BenQayin@ymail.com
aceBook: S Ben Qayin